DISCOVERING AMERICA

A POSITIVE PERSPECTIVE

DR. JAGADEESH PILLAI

Made with ♥ on the Notion Press Platform
www.notionpress.com

Contents

Contents

Prayer

"Om Bhadram Karnebhih Shrunuyaama DevaahBhadram Pashyemaakshabhiryajatraah SthirairangaistushtuvaamsastanoobhihVyashema Devahitam YadaayuhSwasti Na Indro VridhashravaahSwasti Nah Pooshaa VishwavedaahSwasti Nastaarkshyo ArishtanemihSwasti No Brihaspatir DadhaatuOm Shantih, Shantih, Shantih"

The literal meaning of this mantra is: OM. O Gods! Let us hear auspicious words from our ears. O reverent Gods! Let us behold propitious visions from our eyes, let our organs and body be stable, healthy, and strong. Let us do that which is pleasing to the gods in the life span allotted to us. May Indra, inscribed in the scriptures, bring us fortune! May Pushan, the knower of the world, grant us prosperity! May Trakshya, who vanquishes enemies, bestow us with blessings! May Brihaspati bring us success!
OM Peace, Peace, Peace.

About The Author

Dr. Jagadeesh Pillai is a renowned Guinness World Record holder, writer, and researcher hailing from Varanasi, also known as the abode of Lord Shiva. With a Ph.D. in Vedic Science and a range of creative ideas and achievements, he is a true polymath. He is the author of more than 100 books including Research Publications. Although his roots can be traced back to Kerala, the people of Varanasi hold him in high regard and affectionately consider him one of their own.

Dr. Pillai has achieved four Guinness World Records in the following subjects:

"Script to Screen" - In this record, Dr. Pillai produced and directed an animation film within the shortest time possible, breaking the previous record set by Canadians. He has also received numerous national and international awards and recognitions for this achievement.

Longest Line of Postcards - For this record, Dr. Pillai created a line of 16,300 postcards on the occasion of the 163rd anniversary of Indian Postal Day. The event also included a questionnaire about the Indian flag.

Largest Poster Awareness Campaign - Dr. Pillai designed an awareness campaign on the subject of "Beti Bachao - Beti Padhao" (Save the Girl Child - Educate the Girl Child) to achieve this record.

Largest Envelope - In tribute to the Indian Prime Minister's

"Make in India" initiative, Dr. Pillai created a 4000 square meter envelope using waste paper to achieve this record.

Attempted - **70000 Candles on a 210 kg Cake** - To celebrate the 70th Indian Independence Day, Dr. Pillai attempted to light 70,000 candles on a 210 kg cake, which was recorded in World Records India.

Attempted - **Documentary on Dhamek Stupa of Sarnath in 17 Languages** - Dr. Pillai attempted to create a documentary on the Dhamek Stupa of Sarnath, dubbing it in 17 different languages. The result of this attempt is currently awaiting confirmation from the Guinness World Records.

Dr. Pillai is skilled in teaching the Bhagavad Gita, a Hindu scripture, and is popular among young people. He has helped many young people improve their lives through his motivational teachings.

In addition to teaching, he has composed and sung numerous Sanskrit Bhajans and patriotic songs.

He has also written and directed several short films and documentaries for awareness campaigns, and has volunteered with the police in both UP and Kerala to spread awareness about various issues through videos and photography.

Incredibly, he has produced and directed over 100 documentaries about the city of Varanasi, all on his own.

He has also helped and guided more than 25 boys and girls to achieve world records through creative and innovative methods. He is a multifaceted person who uses his intellect and the blessings given to him by God to excel in various areas. He is both a teacher and a student, always learning and teaching, and is able to master any subject he comes across.

He is a selfless social activist and motivational speaker who has overcome struggles and failures to become a successful and enthusiastic individual with a rich life experience.

In addition to his work with the Bhagavad Gita, he is also an efficient Tarot card reader, Astro-Vastu consultant, and a talented singer and composer. He has sung the entire Ram Charita Manas and Bhagavad Gita in his own compositions, and has sung the phrase "Lokah Samastha Sukhino Bhavantu" in 50 different languages. He is currently working on a detailed and scientific study of Vedas, Upanishads, Puranas, and the Bhagavad Gita. He has also composed and sung the Hanuman Chalisa and Gayatri Mantra in 108 and 1008 different compositions, respectively.

Awards - Four Times Guinness World Records, Winner of Mahatma Gandhi Vishwa Shanti Puraskar, Mahatma Gandhi Global Peace Ambassador, Kashi Ratna Award, Dr. APJ Abdul Kalam Motivational Person of the Year 2017, Mother Teresa Award, Indira Gandhi Priyadarshini Award, Bharat Vikas Ratna Award, Udyog Ratna Award, Vigyan Prasar Award, Poorvanchal Ratn Samman.

PREFACE

The United States of America is a country that has played a significant role in shaping the world we live in today. Its rich history, culture, and diversity have made it a fascinating subject for study. This book aims to provide a comprehensive overview of the United States, covering a wide range of topics including culture, economy, education, military, international relations, and future outlook.

The book is divided into chapters that delve into the different aspects of the country, providing a detailed and in-depth examination of each topic. The chapters are written in an easy-to-understand and informative manner, making it accessible for readers of all levels of knowledge and interest.

Whether you are a student, a traveler, or simply someone who is interested in learning more about the United States, this book offers a wealth of information that will deepen your understanding and appreciation of this great nation.

The book is an unbiased and factual representation of the country, it does not include any personal opinions or criticisms. It is a positive and permitted to reveal information only.

We hope that this book will be a valuable resource for anyone looking to learn more about the United States of America.

I

Introduction to the United States of America

The United States of America, often referred to simply as the United States or America, is a federal republic located in North America. It is bordered by Canada to the north, Mexico to the south, and the Atlantic and Pacific Oceans to the east and west. With a population of over 328 million, the United States is the third most populous country in the world and is made up of 50 states and the District of Columbia.

The United States has a rich history that dates back to the late 1700s, when the 13 British colonies in North America declared their independence from British rule. The Declaration of Independence, written by Thomas Jefferson and adopted by the Continental Congress on July 4, 1776, set the foundation for the country's political system and values.

The United States is known for its diverse population, which is made up of people from all over the world. The country is home to a wide range of ethnic groups, including White, African American, Native American, Asian, and Hispanic. The United States is also a melting pot of cultures, with a rich blend of different customs, languages, and traditions.

The United States has a strong economy that is driven by its powerful agricultural, manufacturing, and service sectors. The country is a leader in technology and innovation, and is home to many of the world's top companies and brands. The United States is also a major player in international trade, and has a long history of global commerce and diplomacy.

The United States is a country with a great deal to offer, from its natural beauty and rich history to its diverse population and thriving economy. It is a land of opportunity, where people from all over the world come to pursue their dreams and build a better life. In this book, we will explore the many positive aspects of the United States of America and take a look at what makes this country truly great.

II

The country's Political System and Government

The United States of America has a federal system of government, which means that power is divided between the national government and the individual states. The Constitution of the United States, adopted in 1787, is the supreme law of the land and outlines the structure and powers of the federal government.

The federal government is made up of three branches: the legislative branch, the executive branch, and the judicial branch. The legislative branch, also known as Congress, is made up of two chambers: the Senate and the House of Representatives. The Senate is made up of two senators from each state, while the number of representatives from each state is based on population. Together, Congress is responsible for making and passing laws.

The executive branch is headed by the President of the United States, who is elected every four years by the American people. The President is responsible for enforcing the laws passed by Congress, negotiating treaties with foreign countries, and serving as the commander-in-chief of the armed forces.

The judicial branch is made up of the Supreme Court and lower federal courts. The Supreme Court is the highest court in the land and has the power to interpret the Constitution and make decisions that can affect the entire country. The lower federal courts are responsible for hearing cases that involve federal laws and disputes between states.

The United States also has a system of checks and balances, which means that each branch of government has the power to limit the actions of the other branches. This helps to ensure that no one branch becomes too powerful and protects the rights of the American people.

The United States also has a presidential-congressional system of government, where the President serves as both head of state and head of government and the Congress legislates. The President is elected by an electoral college and serves for four years.

In addition to the federal government, each state has its own government, with its own constitution, governor, and legislature. The states have significant autonomy and powers, and this federal system allows for a balance of power between the national and state governments.

III

The History of the United States

The history of the United States is rich and complex, spanning over 400 years of exploration, colonization, revolution, and growth.

The first known inhabitants of what is now the United States were Indigenous peoples, who have lived in the Americas for thousands of years before the arrival of European explorers. In 1492, Christopher Columbus, an Italian explorer, set sail under the sponsorship of the Spanish monarchy and landed in the Caribbean, thinking he had reached the East Indies. This led to the beginning of European exploration and colonization of the Americas.

In the early 1600s, the first successful British colony was established at Jamestown, Virginia. This was followed by the founding of other colonies along the Atlantic coast, including the Massachusetts Bay Colony, the Maryland

Colony, and the Carolinas. These colonies were primarily settled by English, Dutch, and French settlers.

In 1763, the British government imposed new taxes on the colonies, leading to rising tensions between the colonies and the British government. In 1776, thirteen of the colonies declared their independence from British rule, and formed a new nation, the United States of America. The Declaration of Independence, written by Thomas Jefferson, set forth the principles of freedom, democracy, and self-government that would become the foundation of the new nation.

The Revolutionary War between the colonies and Great Britain lasted until 1783, when the Treaty of Paris was signed, recognizing the independence of the United States. In 1787, the Constitution of the United States was written and ratified, establishing a federal system of government and outlining the rights and responsibilities of the American people.

In the following years, the United States expanded westward, through the Louisiana Purchase and the Mexican-American War, and became a global power. The country was divided by the Civil War (1861-65) between the North (Union) and the South (Confederate), which was fought over the issues of slavery and states' rights. The North emerged victorious, and slavery was abolished.

Throughout the late 19th and early 20th centuries, the United States experienced rapid industrialization and urbanization, and became a leading economic power. The country also played a key role in World War I and World War II, and emerged as a superpower in the post-war period.

Since then, the United States has been involved in numerous conflicts, including the Cold War, the Korean War, the Vietnam War, and the Gulf War, and has played a leading role in international affairs. The country has also gone through significant social and political changes, including the Civil Rights Movement and the Women's Rights Movement. Today, the United States continues to be a major global economic, political, and military power.

IV

The Country's Diverse Demographics and Ethnic Groups

The United States of America is known for its diverse population, which is made up of people from all over the world. According to the United States Census Bureau, the country's population is made up of the following major ethnic groups:

White: 76.5%

Hispanic or Latino: 18.5%

Black or African American: 13.4%

Asian: 5.9%

Native American and Alaska Native: 2.9%

Native Hawaiian and Pacific Islander: 0.2%

Two or more races: 2.7%

It's important to note that these percentages are approximate and can vary by location.

The white population is primarily of European descent, with the largest ancestry groups being German, Irish, English, and Italian. The Hispanic or Latino population is made up of people of Mexican, Puerto Rican, Cuban, Salvadoran, and Dominican descent, among others. The Black or African American population is primarily of African descent, and the Asian population is made up of people of Chinese, Filipino, Indian, Vietnamese, Korean, and Japanese descent, among others. The Native American and Alaska Native population is made up of people of Indigenous descent.

The United States is also home to a large immigrant population, with over 44 million immigrants in 2019, making up about 13.7% of the total population. The largest countries of origin for immigrants are Mexico, China, India, the Philippines, and El Salvador. Immigrants in the US come from all over the world and add to the diversity of the country.

Due to its history of immigration, the United States is a melting pot of cultures, with a rich blend of different customs, languages, and traditions. This diversity is one of the country's great strengths and is reflected in its art, music, food, and social fabric. The cultural diversity of the country also brings a richness and depth to its society, making it a unique and vibrant place to live.

V

The American Economy and its role in the Global Market

The United States has a capitalist mixed economy, which is one of the largest and most technologically advanced in the world. Its economy is characterized by a high level of innovation, productivity, and economic freedom. The country has a Gross Domestic Product (GDP) of over 21 trillion dollars, making it the world's largest economy.

The American economy is driven by a variety of industries, including agriculture, manufacturing, and services. The country is one of the world's leading producers of grains, fruits, and vegetables, as well as meat and dairy products. The manufacturing sector is also a major contributor to the economy, with the United States being a leading producer of automobiles, machinery, and consumer goods. The services sector, which includes finance, healthcare, and education, is also an important part of the economy and employs the majority of the American workforce.

The United States is also a major player in the global market, with exports and imports playing a significant role in the economy. The country is one of the world's leading exporters of agricultural products, manufactured goods, and services. It also imports a wide range of goods and services from around the world.

The American economy is also characterized by a high level of innovation and entrepreneurship, with many of the world's leading companies and brands being based in the United States. The country is also home to some of the world's top universities and research institutions, which drive innovation and technological advancement.

The Federal Reserve (Fed) is the central bank of the United States, responsible for implementing monetary policy. The Fed uses a variety of tools, such as setting interest rates, to influence the economy and stabilize prices.

The United States is also a member of several international economic organizations, such as the World Trade Organization (WTO) and the International Monetary Fund (IMF), which helps to promote free trade and economic cooperation among countries.

Overall, the American economy plays a critical role in the global market and its stability and growth have a significant impact on the world economy.

VI

The Education System and Opportunities for Higher Learning

The United States has a highly developed education system that offers a wide range of opportunities for higher learning. The education system is primarily the responsibility of individual states and local communities, with the federal government playing a limited role.

The American education system is divided into three levels: primary, secondary, and post-secondary. Primary and secondary education, also known as K-12 education, is compulsory for all children between the ages of 5 and 18. Public schools are the most common form of primary and secondary education in the United States, although there are also private and parochial schools.

After completing secondary education, students have the option to attend post-secondary education, which includes vocational schools, community colleges, and universities. The United States is home to some of the world's top universities, including Harvard, Stanford, and the Massachusetts Institute of Technology (MIT), which are known for their academic excellence and research.

Higher education in the United States is diverse, and provides a wide range of options for students. Community colleges offer two-year associate degrees and vocational programs, while four-year colleges and universities offer undergraduate and graduate degrees in a variety of fields, such as business, engineering, medicine, and law.

The United States also offers opportunities for international students to study in the country. Many American universities have robust international student populations and provide support services to help students adjust to life in the United States.

The American education system is widely considered to be one of the best in the world, offering students a wide range of opportunities for higher learning and personal growth. It is known for its academic excellence, research opportunities and its ability to provide students with the skills and knowledge they need to succeed in their chosen fields.

VII

The Arts and Literature of the United States

The arts and literature of the United States are diverse and reflect the country's rich cultural heritage. American art and literature have been shaped by the experiences of the country's diverse population and have had a significant impact on the world.

In the field of visual arts, the United States has produced many renowned artists, such as the abstract expressionists Jackson Pollock, Mark Rothko and Willem de Kooning, the pop artist Andy Warhol, the realist painter Edward Hopper, and the modernist photographer Ansel Adams. The country is also home to many world-renowned museums, such as the Metropolitan Museum of Art and the Smithsonian American Art Museum, which showcase American and international art.

In literature, the United States has produced many famous and influential authors, such as Nathaniel Hawthorne, Edgar Allan Poe, Mark Twain, Ernest Hemingway, and F. Scott Fitzgerald. American literature is known for its realism, its exploration of the human condition and its ability to reflect the nation's cultural diversity. The United States has also produced many influential poets, such as Walt Whitman, Emily Dickinson, Langston Hughes, and Maya Angelou.

In the field of music, the United States is known for its diverse and dynamic music scene. American music has had a profound influence on the world, from jazz, blues, and rock and roll to hip-hop, country, and R&B. Many American musicians, such as Louis Armstrong, Duke Ellington, Bob Dylan, and Bruce Springsteen, have become cultural icons and have had a significant impact on the world of music.

In theater, the United States has produced many acclaimed playwrights, such as Tennessee Williams, Arthur Miller and August Wilson, and have had Broadway as a major center for theatrical performances.

In cinema, the United States has produced many influential films and filmmakers, such as Orson Welles, Martin Scorsese and Steven Spielberg, and Hollywood has become the global center for the film industry.

Overall, the arts and literature of the United States are diverse, dynamic, and have had a significant impact on the world. The country's rich cultural heritage is reflected in its art, literature, music, theater, and cinema, which continue to inspire and influence people around the globe.

VIII

The Country's Delicious Cuisine and Traditional Foods

The United States is known for its diverse and delicious cuisine, which reflects the country's rich cultural heritage. American cuisine is a melting pot of different culinary traditions, with influences from various ethnic groups, including European, African, Asian, and Indigenous peoples.

One of the most popular American dishes is the hamburger, which is believed to have originated in the late 19th century. Another classic American dish is the hot dog, a grilled or steamed sausage that is traditionally served in a bun.

Regional cuisines in the United States also vary widely.

Southern cuisine is known for its hearty, flavorful dishes, such as fried chicken, barbecue, and grits. Tex-Mex cuisine, which originated in Texas and the Mexican border regions, is a fusion of Mexican and American flavors, and is known for dishes such as chili con carne, fajitas, and Tex-Mex style tacos. New Orleans cuisine is famous for its Creole and Cajun dishes, such as gumbo, jambalaya and po'boys.

The United States is also known for its diverse seafood dishes, such as crab cakes, lobster, and clam chowder. The country's Pacific Northwest region is particularly famous for its salmon and oyster dishes.

In addition to traditional American dishes, the United States is home to a wide variety of international cuisine, including Chinese, Italian, Mexican, and Indian food, which have become popular in the country.

Additionally, the United States is also known for its sweet treats and desserts, such as apple pie, chocolate chip cookies, and ice cream. The country has a long tradition of baking, and many regional specialties exist such as the New England's Boston cream pie, and the Southern's pecan pie.

The United States is also a major producer of wine and beer, with many regions in the country having their own unique wine and beer styles. California is one of the most famous wine regions in the country, known for its Napa and Sonoma valleys, which produce world-renowned wines. The Pacific Northwest region is also famous for its craft beer scene, with many local breweries producing a wide range of beer styles.

In recent years, the United States has also seen a growing interest in farm-to-table and sustainable food movements, with many restaurants and farmers markets featuring locally-sourced and organic ingredients.

Overall, the cuisine of the United States is diverse, delicious, and reflective of the country's cultural heritage. The country's varied regional and ethnic cuisines, along with its sweet treats and beverages, have something to offer for everyone and continues to evolve with time.

IX

Sports and Recreation in the United States

Sports and recreation play a significant role in American culture and society. The United States is home to a wide variety of sports and recreational activities, from traditional team sports to outdoor activities and fitness.

The most popular sport in the United States is American football, which is played at both the high school and college level, as well as in the professional National Football League (NFL). Basketball and baseball are also popular sports, and are played at both the amateur and professional level. Ice hockey and soccer are also gaining popularity in the country.

The United States is also known for its college sports, with many universities fielding competitive teams in a variety of sports. College football and basketball are particularly popular and attract a large following.

The United States is also home to many major professional sports leagues, including the NFL, the National Basketball Association (NBA), the National Hockey League (NHL), and Major League Baseball (MLB). The country also hosts several major sporting events, such as the Super Bowl, the World Series, and the NCAA Men's Basketball Tournament, which draw large audiences and attract significant media coverage.

Outdoor activities and fitness are also popular in the United States, with many people participating in activities such as hiking, camping, fishing, and skiing. The country is home to many national parks and other protected areas, which offer opportunities for outdoor recreation and adventure.

Overall, sports and recreation play an important role in American culture and society, with a wide range of options and opportunities for people of all ages and interests to stay active, healthy and enjoy their time.

X

The United States' Infrastructure and Transportation System

The United States has a highly developed infrastructure and transportation system that supports the country's economy and connects its people and businesses.

The country has a vast network of roads, highways, and bridges, which connect major cities and rural areas. The federal government, through the Federal Highway Administration, provides funding and sets standards for the country's roads and highways. The country also has a system of limited-access roads, such as the Interstate Highway System, which connects major cities and facilitates long-distance travel.

The United States also has an extensive public transportation system, which includes buses, subways, and light rail in major cities, and commuter rail in some regions. The country's public transportation system is operated by a mix of public and private entities, and is designed to provide affordable and efficient transportation options for the population.

The United States is also home to a large and diverse aviation system, which includes commercial airlines, cargo carriers, and general aviation. The Federal Aviation Administration (FAA) is responsible for the regulation and oversight of the country's aviation system. The country has many major airports, such as Hartsfield-Jackson Atlanta International Airport, Chicago O'Hare International Airport, and Los Angeles International Airport, which serve as hubs for domestic and international travel.

The country's infrastructure also includes a vast network of pipelines and ports, which support the country's energy and trade industries. The United States has a large and modern system of ports, including the Port of Los Angeles, the Port of New York and New Jersey, and the Port of Houston, which handle a large volume of domestic and international cargo.

Overall, the United States has a highly developed infrastructure and transportation system that supports the country's economy and connects its people and businesses. The country's roads, highways, public transportation, aviation, pipelines, and ports are critical to the country's economic and social well-being and play a vital role in connecting the nation.

XI

The Country's Natural Resources and Environment

The United States is rich in natural resources, which include minerals, forests, water, and wildlife. The country's diverse landscapes, including mountains, deserts, forests, and coastlines, also provide a wide range of recreational opportunities and support a variety of ecosystems.

The United States has a diverse mineral industry, which includes the mining of coal, natural gas, oil, gold, silver, and other minerals. The country is also a major producer of industrial minerals, such as sand, gravel, and limestone. These minerals are used in a wide range of industries, including energy, construction, and manufacturing.

The country's forests, which cover over 700 million acres, are a major source of wood and paper products. The United

States has a large and well-developed forest products industry, which includes the harvesting of timber, the production of paper and paper products, and the manufacture of furniture and other wood products.

The United States is also home to a wide variety of wildlife, including many species of mammals, birds, fish, and reptiles. The country's national parks and wildlife refuges provide important habitats for many of these species and offer opportunities for wildlife viewing and recreational activities.

The country also has a vast network of waterways, including rivers and lakes, which are used for transportation, irrigation, and hydroelectric power generation. The Great Lakes, for example, are the largest group of freshwater lakes in the world and provide important resources for the region's economy, recreation, and environment.

The United States' environment is also facing many challenges, including pollution, climate change, and loss of biodiversity. The country's air and water quality have improved in recent decades, but there are still areas of concern, such as air pollution in major cities, and water pollution in certain areas. Climate change is also posing a significant challenge to the country, as rising temperatures and sea levels are affecting many regions and ecosystems.

Overall, the United States' natural resources and environment are diverse and provide many benefits to the country's economy and society. These resources also face many challenges, and efforts are being made to balance the use of these resources with the need to protect and preserve them for future generations.

XII

The American Tourism Industry and Major Attractions

The tourism industry in the United States is a major contributor to the country's economy and is known for its diverse range of attractions and experiences. The United States is one of the most visited countries in the world, with millions of domestic and international tourists visiting each year.

One of the most popular tourist destinations in the United States is the city of New York, which is known for its iconic landmarks such as the Statue of Liberty, Central Park, and the Empire State Building. Other popular cities for tourists include Las Vegas, known for its casinos and entertainment, and San Francisco, known for its cultural attractions and scenic beauty.

The United States is also home to many national parks, which offer visitors the opportunity to experience the country's natural beauty and wildlife. Some of the most popular national parks include Yellowstone, Yosemite, and the Grand Canyon.

The country is also known for its beaches and coastal regions, such as Florida's Miami and The Keys, and Hawaii's Waikiki and Maui. These beaches offer visitors the opportunity to enjoy the sun, sand, and surf and are popular destinations for domestic and international tourists.

The country is also known for its theme parks, such as Walt Disney World in Florida and Universal Studios Hollywood in California, which attract millions of visitors each year.

The United States is also famous for its diverse culture and history, which can be explored through its many museums, historical sites, and landmarks. Some of the most popular cultural and historical attractions include the Smithsonian Institution in Washington D.C., the Kennedy Space Center, and the National Museum of American History.

Overall, the United States' tourism industry is diverse, with a wide range of attractions and experiences that appeal to visitors of all ages and interests. From iconic cities and natural wonders, to beaches and theme parks, the country offers something for everyone. The country's history, culture, and landmarks also offer a glimpse into the nation's past and are a major draw for tourists.

Additionally, the country's diverse regions, from the East Coast to the West Coast, from the North to the South, offer a wide range of landscapes and climate that allow visitors to have a unique experience. The country's tourism industry continues to evolve and adapt to the changing needs and preferences of visitors, making it a popular destination for both domestic and international tourists.

XIII

The United States' Contributions to Technology and Innovation

The United States has a long history of contributions to technology and innovation, which have had a significant impact on the world. American inventors, scientists, and engineers have been responsible for many groundbreaking developments in a wide range of fields, including information technology, biotechnology, energy, transportation, and aerospace.

In the field of information technology, the United States has been a leader in the development of computers, software, and the internet. American inventors and engineers have been responsible for many of the key innovations in the field of computers, including the development of the first electronic computer, the UNIVAC, in 1951, and the development of the personal computer in the 1970s. American companies such as Apple, Microsoft, and Google have also been major players in the development of the internet and the world wide web.

In the field of biotechnology, American scientists and researchers have made significant contributions to the understanding of genetics and the development of new medical treatments. The Human Genome Project, an international effort to map the human genome, was led by American scientists and was completed in 2003. American biotech companies have also developed a wide range of new drugs and medical treatments, including many of the most widely used drugs for cancer, diabetes, and other diseases.

In the field of energy, American inventors and engineers have made significant contributions to the development of new energy technologies, including the development of the first commercial nuclear power plant in the 1950s, and the development of shale gas and fracking technologies in recent years.

In the field of transportation, American inventors and engineers have made significant contributions to the development of new transportation technologies, including the development of the first commercial jetliner, the Boeing 707, in the 1950s, and the development of the first hybrid and electric cars in recent years.

In the field of aerospace, American inventors and engineers have made significant contributions to the development of new aerospace technologies, including the development of the first successful liquid-fueled rocket, the first aircraft to fly faster than the speed of sound, and the first spacecraft to land on the Moon.

Overall, the United States has a long and rich history of contributions to technology and innovation, which have had a significant impact on the world and continue to shape the way we live today. American scientists, engineers, and inventors have been responsible for many of the most important technological and scientific advances of the past century and continue to push the boundaries of what is possible.

XIV

The country's Famous People and Notable Figures

The United States has produced a number of famous people and notable figures throughout its history, across many different fields, including politics, entertainment, literature, sports, and science.

In the field of politics, the United States has produced many notable figures, including George Washington, the first President of the United States; Abraham Lincoln, who led the country during the Civil War and abolished slavery; Franklin D. Roosevelt, who served as President during the Great Depression and World War II; and Barack Obama, the first African American President of the United States.

In the field of entertainment, the United States has produced many famous actors, musicians, and entertainers, including actors such as Marlon Brando, Audrey Hepburn, and Tom Hanks; musicians such as Louis Armstrong, Elvis Presley, and Michael Jackson; and entertainers such as Fred Astaire, Lucille Ball, and Oprah Winfrey.

In the field of literature, the United States has produced many famous authors and poets, including Ernest Hemingway, J.D. Salinger, and Toni Morrison; and poets such as Robert Frost, Langston Hughes, and Maya Angelou.

In the field of sports, the United States has produced many famous athletes, including Michael Jordan, Babe Ruth, and Muhammad Ali; and coaches such as Vince Lombardi, Phil Jackson and Pat Summitt.

In the field of science, the United States has produced many famous scientists, inventors, and engineers, including Thomas Edison, Alexander Graham Bell, and the Wright Brothers; and scientists such as Albert Einstein, Stephen Hawking and Marie Curie.

Overall, the United States has produced many famous people and notable figures throughout its history, across many different fields, who have had a significant impact on the world and continue to be remembered and celebrated today.

XV

American Culture and Social Customs

American culture is diverse and complex, reflecting the country's history and the many different groups of people who have settled there. American culture encompasses a wide range of customs, beliefs, and traditions, including those of Indigenous peoples, European colonizers, African slaves, and immigrants from around the world.

One of the key aspects of American culture is its emphasis on individualism and freedom. Americans place a high value on personal liberty and the ability to pursue one's own goals and dreams. This emphasis on individualism is reflected in many aspects of American culture, including the country's political system, which is based on the principles of democracy and the rule of law.

American culture is also characterized by its melting pot of different cultures and traditions. This diversity is reflected in the country's food, music, and art, which have been influenced by the many different groups of people who have settled in the United States. American cuisine, for example, is a melting pot of different culinary traditions, with influences from various ethnic groups, including European, African, Asian, and Indigenous peoples.

Another key aspect of American culture is its relationship to consumerism and materialism. Americans have a strong culture of consumption and are known for their love of shopping and material possessions. This culture of consumerism is reflected in the country's advertising, marketing, and retail industries, which play a major role in the American economy.

Social customs in the United States vary depending on the region and the community, but Americans are generally considered to be friendly, outgoing and easy-going people. Americans are also known for their love of celebrations, particularly holidays such as Thanksgiving and Christmas. American culture is also characterized by a strong sense of community, with many people participating in civic and social organizations, such as sports teams, clubs, and churches.

Overall, American culture is diverse and complex, reflecting the country's history and the many different groups of people who have settled there. American culture encompasses a wide range of customs, beliefs, and traditions, including those of Indigenous peoples, European colonizers, African slaves, and immigrants from around the world.

XVI

The United States' Education System and Literacy Rates

The education system in the United States is diverse and complex, with many different levels and types of institutions. The system is primarily funded and administered by state and local governments, with some federal oversight.

The education system in the United States typically includes:

Public schools: These are government-funded schools that are open to all students and are required to follow certain curriculum guidelines and standards set by the state or local government.

Private schools: These are schools that are typically not government-funded and have more flexibility in terms of curriculum and standards. Some private schools are religious or have a specific focus, such as Montessori or Waldorf education.

Higher education: This includes colleges and universities that offer undergraduate and graduate degrees. The United States has a wide range of colleges and universities, including community colleges, state universities, and prestigious private universities.

The literacy rate in the United States is relatively high, with an estimated 99% of adults aged 25 and over having the ability to read and write. However, there are disparities in literacy rates among different groups of people, with lower rates among certain populations, such as those living in poverty or those with limited English proficiency.

The education system in the United States has faced many challenges in recent years, including lack of funding, inadequate resources, and a lack of access to high-quality education for some students. Efforts are being made to address these issues and to improve the education system for all students.

Overall, the United States' education system and literacy rates are relatively high, but there are still disparities and challenges that need to be addressed in order to ensure that all students have access to a high-quality education.

XVII

American Trade and Commerce

The United States has one of the most developed and largest economies in the world, with a highly diversified and sophisticated system of trade and commerce. American trade and commerce is characterized by its openness to foreign markets and investment, its high levels of productivity and innovation, and its ability to adapt to changing economic conditions.

The United States is a major player in the global economy, and its businesses and industries are involved in a wide range of trade and commerce activities, including exporting and importing goods and services, foreign direct investment, and technology transfer.

The United States is one of the largest exporters in the world, with exports of goods and services totaling over $2 trillion in 2020. The country's major exports include industrial and agricultural products, high-tech goods, and services such as finance, transportation, and education. The United States is also one of the largest importers in the world, with imports totaling over $2.7 trillion in 2020. The country's major imports include manufactured goods, oil, and consumer goods.

The United States is also a major player in the global service sector, with a large and sophisticated service industry that includes finance, business services, transportation, and telecommunications. American businesses and industries are also major investors abroad, with American foreign direct investment totaling over $4 trillion in 2020.

The United States is also a member of many international trade agreements and organizations, such as the World Trade Organization (WTO), North American Free Trade Agreement (NAFTA), and the Trans-Pacific Partnership (TPP), which aims to promote trade and investment among member countries.

Overall, American trade and commerce is characterized by its openness to foreign markets and investment, its high levels of productivity and innovation, and its ability to adapt to changing economic conditions. The United States' economy is one of the most developed and largest in the world, and its businesses and industries are involved in a wide range of trade and commerce activities that are critical to the country's economic growth and prosperity.

XVIII

The Country's Military and Defense System

The United States has one of the largest and most advanced military and defense systems in the world. The military is made up of several branches, including the Army, Navy, Air Force, Marine Corps, and Coast Guard. These branches are overseen by the Department of Defense, which is responsible for the overall management and direction of the military.

The United States has a large and well-equipped military, with advanced weapons systems, technology, and equipment. The country also has a large number of active duty and reserve personnel, and a significant defense budget, which is one of the largest in the world.

The United States has a global presence, with military bases and personnel stationed in countries around the world. The country is also involved in a number of military operations and alliances, including the North Atlantic Treaty Organization (NATO) and the United Nations (UN).

The United States' military and defense system is designed to protect the country's national security and interests, both domestically and internationally. The military is responsible for defending the country against potential threats, and providing support and assistance to other countries in the event of a crisis. The military also plays a role in providing humanitarian aid and disaster relief, both domestically and internationally.

The United States military and defense system is also constantly evolving and adapting to changing global conditions and emerging threats. The country is investing in new technologies, such as cyber security, unmanned systems, and hypersonic weapons, to maintain its military advantage.

Overall, the United States' military and defense system is one of the most advanced and powerful in the world, with a large and well-equipped military and a global presence. The military and defense system is responsible for protecting the country's national security and interests, both domestically and internationally. The country's military also plays a role in providing humanitarian aid and disaster relief, both domestically and internationally.

XIX

The United States' International Relations and Diplomacy

The United States has a complex and dynamic system of international relations and diplomacy, which is designed to protect and promote the country's national interests and values on the global stage. The United States has diplomatic relations with countries around the world and is a member of many international organizations, such as the United Nations (UN), the World Trade Organization (WTO), and the World Health Organization (WHO).

The United States' foreign policy is guided by a number of key principles and objectives, including the promotion of democracy and human rights, the defense of national security and the protection of American citizens abroad, and the promotion of economic growth and prosperity.

The United States has a strong and influential presence in the international community, and its foreign policy is shaped by a number of key actors and institutions, including the President, the Department of State, and the United States Congress.

The United States has traditionally had close relationships with many countries in North America, Europe, and Asia, and has played a leading role in the formation of key international organizations such as the United Nations and NATO. The country is also a leading member of the G7, G20, and the World Bank.

The United States' international relations and diplomacy are also shaped by its economic and military power. The country is one of the world's largest trading nations and has a powerful and sophisticated military. The United States is also known for its soft power, which is its ability to attract and co-opt rather than coerce, using its culture, political values, and foreign policies.

In recent years, the United States has had a complex relationship with some of the most significant countries such as China, Russia, and North Korea. The country has also been involved in a number of conflicts and interventions in different regions of the world, including the Middle East, Africa, and Asia.

Overall, the United States' international relations and diplomacy are complex and dynamic, shaped by a number of key principles, actors, and institutions. The country is a major player in the international community and its foreign policy is designed to protect and promote the country's national interests and values on the global stage.

XX

Future Outlook for the United States of America

In conclusion, the United States of America is a diverse and dynamic country with a rich history and culture. The country has a complex and sophisticated system of politics, economy, education, trade and commerce, military and defense, and international relations and diplomacy. The United States has been a leader in many fields and has had a significant impact on the world.

The United States has faced many challenges throughout its history, including economic downturns, social and political divisions, and conflicts. The country has also faced a number of more recent challenges, such as the COVID-19 pandemic, racial and social injustice and political polarization.

Despite these challenges, the United States has a strong and resilient economy, and a diverse and innovative society, which will continue to be a major player on the global stage. The country's political system, democracy, will continue to be a model for many countries around the world. The country's economy is expected to recover and continue to grow in the future. The country will continue to be a leader in innovation and technology, and will continue to play an important role in international trade and diplomacy.

It is expected that the United States will continue to face a number of challenges in the future, including issues related to economic inequality, climate change, and political polarization. However, the country has a strong tradition of resilience and adaptability, and it is likely that the United States will continue to be a major player on the global stage for many years to come.

Other Books Of The Author

1. The Moments When I Met God
2. Kashiyile Theertha Pathangal
3. GURU GYAN VANI
4. Abhiprerak Gita
5. ASSI SE JAIN GHAT TAK
6. Hopelessness of Arjuna
7. The Soul and It's True Nature
8. Sense of Action (Karma)
9. Action through Wisdom
10. Action through Wisdom
11. THEORY AND PRACTICAL OF EVERY ACTION
12. LOGICAL UNDERSTANDING OF THE SUPREME
13. THE IMPERISHABLE SUPREME
14. Yatra Nishadraj se Hanuman Ghat Tak
15. Yatra Karnatak Ghat se Raja Ghat Tak
16. Yatra Pandey Ghat se Prayagraj Ghat Tak
17. Yatra Ranjendra Prasad Ghat se Dattatreya Ghat Tak
18. YaatraSindhiya Ghat se Gwaliar Ghat Tak
19. Yatra Mangala Gauri Ghat se Hanuman Gadhi Ghat Tak
20. Yatra Gaay Ghat Se Nishad Ghat Tak
21. MAA GANGA, GHATEN EVM UTSAV
22. Ganga Arti Dev Deepavali evam Any Utsav
23. Potentials of Digitalized India
24. VEDIC CONSCIOUSNESS
25. A Brief Introduction to Vedic Science
26. Kashi ke Barah Jyotirling
27. IMPACT OF MOTIVATION
28. Let's have a Milky Way Journey
29. Color Therapy in a Nutshell

30. Rigveda in a Nutshell
31. Yajurveda in a Nutshell
32. Samveda in a Nutshell
33. Atharva Veda in a Nutshell
34. Ayushman Bhava - Ayurveda
35. Srimad Bhagavad Gita and Upanishad Connection
36. Srimad Bhagavad Gita - an attempt to summarize each chapter.
37. Facts and Impact of Nakshatra
38. Astro Gems - NAVARATNA
39. Ekadashi - A Concise Overview
40. A Concise View of Hanuman Chalisa
41. Inspirational Gita
42. Nakshatraranyam
43. Summary of 18 Mahapuranas
44. Synopsis of 18 Upa Puranas
45. Rigvediya Upanishads
46. Shukla Yajurvediya Upanishads
47. Krishna Yajurvediya Upanishads
48. Samavediya Upanishads
49. Atharvavediya Upanishads
50. The Seven Great Sages
51. From Rocket Scientist to President Dr. APJ Abdul Kalam
52. The Visionary's Voice - Quotes of Dr. APJ Abdul Kalam
53. The Wisdom of Swami Vivekananda: Insights and Inspiration from a Legendary Spiritual Teacher
54. Ayurvedic Remedies from the Garden
55. Sages and Seers
56. Rising Strong – Motivational Stories of Women
57. Beyond Flames -Mystery stories of Funeral Ghat Manikarnika
58. The Origins of Tulsi: A Look at the Mythological Roots of the Plant"

59. The Holistic Cow: A Look at the Physical, Spiritual, and Cultural Importance of Cows in India
60. Arts of Healing
61. Exploring the Divine
62. Understanding Five Elements
63. The Etymology of Ram
64. Symbols of India
65. Voice of Change (About Speeches of Great Men)
66. She Speaks (About Speeches of Great Women)
67. Patriotism on Celluloid – Brief About Patriotic Films
68. The Music of Motivation: A Brief Guide to Inspirational Film Songs
69. **Unlocking the Secrets of the Dashopanishads**
70. A Cultural Mosaic
71. Ancient Traditions, Modern Minds
72. Ecos of Ancient Wisdom
73. Beneath the Surface
74. From Temples to Ashrams
75. Sages of the Subcontinent
76. The Art of Healling (Ayurveda, Yoga & Naturopathy)
77. Indian Kitchen
78. The Festivals of India
79. The Indian Epics Retold
80. The Power of Mantras
81. The Indian River Ganges
82. The Indian Architecture
83. Rites of Passage
84. The Indian Silk Road
85. The Indian Literature
86. The Indian Villages
87. The Indian Folks & Crafts
88. The Way of Buddha
89. The Ramayan of Tulsidas

90. Astrological Remedies
91. The Secret Power of Motivation
92. Secret of Developing your Inner Strength
93. The Secret Path to Motivation
94. The Art and Secret of Positive Thinking
95. The Secrets of Practicing Ethical Living
96. Indian Art and Painting
97. The Indian Herbalism
98. The Palette of India
99. Bharatanatyam to Kathak
100. Exploring India's Astrological Remedies
101. The Indian Festival of Flowers
102. Indian Handicrafts
103. The Splashes of Joy – India's Colour Festival
104. The Indian Science of Astrology
105. The Indian Mythology
106. Path to Enlightenment
107. The Indian Spirituality for Children
108. Aromas of India
109. The Secrets of Healthy Relationships
110. The Indian Street Food
111. Discovering America
112. The Indian Street Food

Contact

DR. JAGADEESH PILLAI

PhD in Vedic Science

Four Times Guinness World Record Holder

Winner of Mahatma Gandhi Vishwa Shanti Puraskar and Global Peace Ambassador

Gemology, Astro & Vastu Consultant - Spiritual Counselor

Consultant for designing World Record Ideas

Efficient Tarot Card Reader

9839093003

myrichindia@gmail.com

drjagadeeshpillai@facebook

drjagadeeshpillai@instagram

jagadeeshpillai@youtube

www. JAGADEESHPILLAI.com

|| LOKAHA SAMASTHAHA SUKHINO BHAVANTU ||

Printed by Libri Plureos GmbH in Hamburg, Germany